Caregivers

Study Guide for The Unsung Heroes of Our Day

Offering support, encouragement and hope to caregivers and their families

Dr. Tom and Dawn Randall

Copyright 2017

Property of Dr. Thomas E.   &   Dawn Randall

No part of this publication may be reproduced, stored in a retrieval system, or transmitted, in any form or by any means - electronic, mechanical, photocopying, recording or otherwise - without prior written permission.

All Scripture quotations, except where indicated, are taken from the New International Version, copyright 2005. Zondervan, Grand Rapids, Michigan.

Caregivers: Study Guide for
The Unsung Heroes of Our Day

Offering hope, encouragement and support to caregivers and their families

Welcome to the study guide for *Caregivers: The Unsung Heroes of Our Day* and the work of **A Touch of Hope Ministries.** Adjusting to being a caregiver eventually and hopefully involves recognizing the need to accept support, validation and even relief for yourself, your disabled family member and your family. It implies the need for a trusted confidant and support network. New friendships with those who understand, as every caregiver learns, are beyond value. It is our goal that each caregiver's support group seeks to build these connections that ultimately extend beyond the sessions into relationships that become long-term friendships.

This study guide is a companion study to *Caregivers: The Unsung Heroes of Our Day* and together they serve the purpose of encouraging participants as they face the challenges and complexities associated with being caregivers. What presents the need for someone being a caregiver usually involves a family member contending with a disability, chronic pain or a debilitating or terminal illness, any of which intensifies the pressures upon a home and family.

Further enrichment can be gained by joining or starting a support group designed to offer hope and guidance by providing an atmosphere of support and encouragement as they look through the eyes of a caregiver in learning how to handle adversity. Often overlooked and often just expected to respond to a loved one's crisis, caregivers find themselves drawn into intense situations that bring with them another set of circumstances that require their attention. The importance of this kind of group comes to life in helping to address the often-unseen pressures that confront the caregiver, in addition to the perplexities that confront the one needing care.

About A Touch of Hope Ministries

A Touch of Hope Ministries formed out of the need to address the complexities being faced by many who awake each day as a caregiver. Following Pastor Tom Randall's doctoral thesis, which addressed the issues of caregiving, physical disability and the church's place in caring for families who contend with these issues, A Touch of Hope Ministries was born to offer support and hope to caregivers and their families.

Dr. Tom brings to the discussion his 40 plus years' experience in the pastoral counseling and teaching ministry in addition to his 25 plus years as a caregiver to his best friend and wife, Dawn. Together with Dawn they have taught marriage and family classes for 30 of those years and now have directed their unmistakable passions to encourage families facing perplexing issues as they have.

Tom and Dawn serve as the directors to A Touch of Hope Ministries. Tom also presently serves as the Care Pastor at a church in Gilbert, Arizona. His responsibilities entail crises and pastoral counseling, training of chaplains that serve in the Care and Support Ministries of the church, as well as other teaching responsibilities and providing pastoral care and oversight in this growing church of approximately 4000 people.

Tom together with Dawn began their ministry in Bellingham, Washington, where Tom was a pastor for 30 years. They then moved and pastored in Ridgefield, Washington while Tom pursued his doctorate before moving to Gilbert, AZ. Tom is a graduate of Washington State University with a Bachelor of Science in Civil Engineering. He then acquired his Master of Divinity (1976) and his doctorate (2011) from Western Seminary in Portland, Oregon. His dissertation addressed the issues of caregiving, physical disability and the church's place in caring for families who contend with these issues. His book His book, *Caregivers: The Unsung Heroes of Our Day*, lays a foundation to the ministry of A Touch of Hope Ministries.

Dawn received a Bachelor's of Science degree in Bacteriology and Public Health from W.S.U. and was a medical technologist. Dawn has also been physically disabled since 1991. Complications from two automotive accidents necessitated a series of surgeries that has left her disabled and contending with severe, chronic pain. They are parents of two sons, two daughters plus Papa and Nana to ten grandchildren.

In addition to the Randalls, A Touch of Hope Ministries has other qualified counselors who serve on their ministry team. A brief biography and contact information can be obtained at the website, atouchofhopeministries. com. As an added resource, a webinar video series has been developed for classroom and group studies.

Caring and Learning to Handle Adversity

For sure, learning how to handle adversity will face each person at some point in life. Yet, with a disability or situation that results in a disability, chronic pain, suffering or even terminal illness, matters of one's heart and relationship with loved ones, as well as God, will need to be addressed sooner than later. Forming a frame of mind for making the most of our adversities then becomes a focal point for all those who encounter such tribulations.

Looking through the eyes of the caregiver, this group study will bring to the surface essential areas of concern that accompany adversity and will seek to offer insights and counsel in addressing satisfactorily the matters that confront our relationships when life-altering crises arrive at our doors. It will take into account our relationships, not only with each other, but God, which presents itself with the potential of being a life-changing study.

As mentioned, this workbook goes hand in hand with the webinar materials presented in the sessions and the book, *Caregivers: The Unsung Heroes of Our Day*. Further interaction around the content of the presentations, along with the reading and homework discussions, are all designed to offer healthy insights for strengthening individuals and building encouraging relationships.

How the Caregivers' Support Groups Work

Regular Group Meetings

As many contending with these types of issues find weekly meetings difficult to work into their schedules, our suggestion to which we have found the best results is to meet twice a month or bi-weekly. This allows ample time for the participants to involve themselves in the essential study and interaction, while contending with their hardships. Final discretion is left to each group to determine their particular schedule. We have also utilized online groups for those whose conditions necessitate such need and we found them most adequate in helping participants.

Nature of the Content

The session content recognizes that caregiving necessitates our willingness to redefine and reconstruct our lives, which in turn necessitates the sensitivity and courage to refine and nurture our own inner journey. Therefore, each session focuses upon providing participants with the needed considerations and challenges for understanding and nurturing one's own personal journey. At the same time, caring for the weak implies a call to being an encourager, which undoubtedly becomes a personal quality that throughout the sessions will be gradually refined.

This workbook acts as a personal journal for each participant for use in the support group to capture meaningful insights from the presentations and personal take-away notes from the group that are helpful. In addition, a Homework section, which takes the participant through the book entitled, *Caregivers: The Unsung Heroes of Our Day*, offers further clarity and review of the content with personal questions for each participant to address to his or her situation. Clarifications and review will typically begin each new session.

Nature of the Caregiver's Support Group

Adjusting to being a caregiver eventually and hopefully involves recognizing the need to accept support, validation and even relief for yourself, your disabled family member and your family. It implies the need for a trusted confidant and support network. New friendships with those who understand, as every caregiver learns, are beyond value. The support groups seek to build these connections that ultimately extend beyond the sessions into relationships that become long-term friendships.

Each group is designed to encourage participants in their personal experiences of being caregivers. As mentioned, each meeting includes a time of interaction pertaining to the content of the evening and clarification of questions from homework. A further time of voluntary personal discussion, pertaining to the difficulties and successes of members of the group, is incorporated to help strengthen participants in their own personal challenges.

Nature of the Larger Ministry

The dream for each Caregiver's Support Group is that it grows into a ministry that connects people by offering assistance to those like themselves, who have been pressed to contend with the hardships associated with caregiving. It is also the goal of the ministry leadership team to build *community resource teams* to assist attendees with needed information concerning their situations. This includes building a network of gifted people that becomes available for medical, financial, dietary and spiritual information, as well as qualified assistance to give necessary home assistance and even respite to the caregiver and even the family.

How to Connect to a Caregiver's Support Group

To connect to a group, fill out a registration form and return it to the facilitating leaders of the group. Expect a representative from the group leadership to contact you with information about specific groups that will best accommodate your needs. If your only opportunity to attend a group would be online, and none are available locally, contact A Touch of Hope Ministries.

Caregiver's Support Group Guidelines and Rules

Each support group exists for the purpose of encouraging its participants as they face the challenges and complexities associated with caregiving. This necessitates that this group operates within a safe, confidential, and healthy environment, which lends to the growth of its participants and their families.

Honor Confidentiality

What happens or is shared within the group must stay within the group. This protects the opportunity for unnecessary or hurtful information reaching someone outside the group who may be affected by the information shared. Confidentiality provides an atmosphere for developing trust between the support group members and leaders. * (See Confidentiality Agreement below.)

Be Open

Learning to listen and learning to express oneself honestly within the group is necessary for the personal success of each participant and the group. An assurance of acceptance opens the pathway to true transformation within individuals. There is no requirement that one talks within the group, though it is strongly encouraged. Our intent is to accept and encourage each other and to avoid making judgments.

Respect One Another

As different personalities express themselves differently, be sensitive to allow each participant the opportunity to speak without interruptions. Take into account the time, so that each participant has ample time to interact. Courtesy implies listening to the one speaking without holding secondary conversations with others, while someone is sharing. Let one's comments be brief, to the point, and directed to the topic at hand.

Please understand that in this group cell phones are allowed to be on for many caregivers are on call to handle emergencies from those for whom they are caregivers. If this is the case, we ask the one receiving the call quietly exit the group meeting to address the call. It would also be appropriate to inform the group upon your return of the nature of the call, and if need be to pray for the situation.

Support the Group Process

Each participant enters the group from a situation in which they have already been in personally. Accept participants where they are and offer the support necessary to encourage them in coping and growing through the challenges they face. Refrain from criticizing any professional counsel a participant has received outside the group.

Consider Others as More Important than Yourself (Philippians 2:3)

This Caregiver's Group is a Christ-centered support network that seeks to encourage every participant in their meetings. There is no place for offensive or abusive language within the group. We know the Scriptures to teach us all that we "consider others as more important than ourselves," which implies that we place value upon each participant and as a result offer constructive insights that expand one's ability to successfully address each challenge. If a crisis occurs or becomes recognizable, it is the responsibility of the group leader to handle the issue at the appropriate time or even to address the matter outside the group time.

Additional Group Guidelines

- Each group will be guided by a qualified group facilitator. All members will be referred to by their first names.
- Encouraging one another stems from a genuine development of relationships between the group participants. In our conversations, then, we strongly suggest the use of "I" or "me" statements, so that we keep our conversations of a personal nature and avoid making judgmental statements that can create an uncomfortable setting. For example,
    "When that story was shared, I felt so uncomfortable." Not
    "Your story made me feel uncomfortable."
- We have the right to ask questions of each other, not as a platform for debate, but to gain clarity pertaining to the matters at hand. We also have the right to refuse to answer questions, if we do not recognize how our words will benefit the group at that time. "Do

not let any unwholesome talk come out of your mouths, but only what is helpful for building others up according to their needs, that it may benefit those who listen" (Ephesians 4:29).
- One person speaks at a time. The only exception would be to ask for clarity.
- Everyone should have a chance to speak once (or pass) before allowing open interaction on a topic.
- Keep comments brief and directed to the topic or subject matter at hand. Do not attack a person who expresses an opinion.
- Agree to disagree on matters that do not pertain to the group's purpose for existence and the success of each participant.
- Remember, we will all be learning together.

Confidentiality Agreement of the Caregiver's Support Group

Every support group will attempt to keep confidential the information it obtains in the course of their ministry to individuals. Those who participate in our support groups must agree to hold confidential the information they obtain about fellow support group members. We know that protecting member's confidentiality from other members in the group is extremely difficult. We ask that members of the support group not give out information about fellow group members. If one chooses to share that information directly that is acceptable.

* (The only exception to confidentiality is when someone threatens harm to themselves or anyone else. In such cases the need for protecting people takes precedent and the leadership or authorities must be immediately informed to prevent any harmful activity from happening.)

Table of Contents

Caregivers: Study Guide for The Unsung Heroes of Our Day

Welcome iii
How the Caregivers' Support Groups Work vi
Caregiver's Support Group Guidelines and Rules viii

Support Group Sessions

Session 1: In the Shadows: A Caregiver's Story & the Challenges Facing Our Homes, Communities and Churches   1

Session 2: The Unsung Heroes: A Caregiver's Message, Work, Ethic and Rightful Title   6

Session 3: The Four Corners to Puzzling Events 11

Session 4: Corner Piece # 1 (CP#1): When Crises Hit: Adversity's Immediate Effects & Handling the "Why, God?" Question   16

Session 5: At the Heart of Adversity: Man in the Image of God 22

Session 6: What Touches One Touches All: Adverse Effects on the Caregiver, the Family and Marriage & the Call to Encouragement   27

Session 7: Corner Piece # 2 (CP #2): Behind Closed Doors Part 1 - The Non-Negotiables of Caregiving   36

Session 8: Corner Piece # 2 (CP#2): Behind Closed Doors Part II - The Non-Negotiables of Caregiving   43

Session 9: In Sickness and in Health: Best Friends by God's Design 48

Session 10: Corner Piece # 3 (CP#3): The Fingerprints of God 58

Session 11: Corner Piece #4 (CP#4): Let's Make Music: Mobilized to Action   68

Session 12: The Power of Caregiving 78

Support Group Registration Form 83

Session 1: In the Shadows: A Caregiver's Story & the Challenges Facing Our Homes, Communities and Churches

Notes

Inspirational People
- The mixing of "courage" and "determination to overcome adversity" breathes into the atmosphere what we have come to understand as "inspiration."
- Another way we sense this quality of inspiration occurs when we see a blending together of the "strength of human spirit" with "compassion" for others that induces a change within someone to overcome or expand beyond one's limits.
- Many inspirational heroes in life occur because of someone "in the shadows," who, though unnoticed and unseen, extends an encouraging hand in a time of need.

In the Shadows
- People of the world understand that pain and suffering are part of our common language.
- Disabilities and adversity have no boundaries, and their effects extend beyond their immediate victims to those "un-wantingly" conscripted into a service referred to as caregiving.
- Faced with losses and crises of their own, these unheralded heroes find themselves summoned into a service that casts them **"into the shadows"** of another.

Once again, Courage, Determination, Strength of human spirit and Compassion for others mix to ignite a power and love that fuels the downtrodden caregivers with the necessary strength for their journey.

We become caregivers by choice, by default or by obligation;
we assume the role because the alternatives are unacceptable.

Beth McLeod

Caregivers...Study Guide

The Story of One Couple – Dawn and Tom

We Are Not Alone

Disability: a physical or mental impairment that substantially limits one or more of the major life activities of an individual (ADA)
- o **Physical** disabilities: affect a person's ability to move.
- o **Sensory** impairments: affect a person's visual and auditory senses.

- o **Cognitive** disabilities: affect a person's ability to mentally process information.
- o **Emotional** disabilities: affect a person's ability to interact with others.
- **In America Alone**:
  - o 1990 – 43 million disabled / One in Five
  - o 2007 – 58 million = 9.4% of the non-institutionalized population over age 5
  - o 2013 – 12.6% of non-institutionalized population of 312 million – 23% of entire population, which is about 73 million
  - o **Why**? Average life expectancy has increased from 49 in 1900 to 75 today.
  - o The number of people 65 and over is expected to double in next 40 years

Caregiving: the act of providing assistance to someone ill or frail
- **In America**
  - o 2000 – 54 million non-professional /family members or friends. o 2009 – 65 million

As the complexities and demands upon caregivers lengthen into a long-term commitment, it becomes apparent that the caregivers themselves will need and deserve support, validation and spiritual renewal, as they travel their own caregiver's journey.

The Church's Challenge and Opportunity
- The Lord's Nature comes to the aid of the weak and needy - Psalm 113:7-8
- Jesus' Mission - Luke 4:18-19

- Paul's address to the early Christians - I Thessalonians 5:14
- Paul's address to the early church leaders in Ephesus - Acts 20:28, 35

For the church, a phenomenal opportunity presents itself—to help families and communities to care for the weak. And if they can't get to us, then how do we get to them?

Take-Away Thoughts

_____
_____
_____

Homework - Session 1

1. To get introduced to the authors, please read the Introduction and Chapter 1 - In the Shadows to the book, *Caregivers: The Unsung Heroes of Our Day.*

2. **Prepare your story, so you could tell it in the group.** *What is your story?* So often caregivers and even those facing a disability find themselves answering the question, "What happened?" Knowing that the disabled person's story is as much the caregiver's story implies that each person knows the story as "Our Story." Not that we will need to express it with every relationship or even at all, but it is important that one can offer a quick and informative version to the story. The main point is to be able to tell your story. If you are a caregiver, think of events that you recall in your history as a caregiver that have been memorable or that clearly marked your journey as a caregiver.

Use this space to briefly outline your personal story:

_____
_____
_____
_____
_____
_____
_____
_____
_____
_____
_____
_____
_____
_____
_____
_____
_____
_____
_____
_____

3. **Read Chapter 2 – We Are Not Alone** from *Caregivers: The Unsung Heroes of Our Day*. We have already covered this material in the opening session but the importance of the material is to make us aware that we are not alone.
   What additional thoughts or clarifications were helpful from the reading?

   _____
   _____
   _____

Recognize Our Responsibility to Care for the Weak

4. Read Jesus' words in Luke 4:18-19 and Matthew 25:35-40. What concern occupies the Lord as he sets about doing His ministry, and then what does He seek from those who are His followers?

5. What simple command, which so reflects the compassionate Spirit of God, did the Apostle Paul include in his closing statements to the church at Thessalonica in I Thess. 5:14, as well as to the New Testament church leaders in Acts 20:35?

Session 2: The Unsung Heroes: A Caregiver's Message, Work, Ethic and Rightful Title

Notes

The Caregiver's Message: Life is Valuable

- Caregiving is not some project to accomplish. It is not a competition or a philosophical test where once learned, we are granted the privilege to graduate to something else.
- Caregiving makes a statement that matters deeply, especially to its immediate recipient. It says loud and clear that <u>life is valuable</u> and to be honored. It personifies the love of Almighty God by its initiating action that supplies another's need.

The Caregiver's Work: A Very Present Help in Trouble

Tears are the glue of the soul. When you weep with a friend, you bind your heart to theirs.

Shelly Beach

- So welcome to the front lines, where people hurt, including even the one who is often administering the care. Let's accept the fact that caregiving and ease are not synonymous.
- For the most part it means rolling up one's own sleeves and jumping into the fray.
    - It is a <u>soul-crunching work,</u> as one's inner make-up is taxed by the often menial, but essential, requirements.
    - It is s<u>pirit-bending</u>, as the wrestling within one's heart to make sense of one's plight simultaneously competes with the necessity of loving another as Christ would.
    - Called to care, called to love, called to be a true friend, the work becomes a personification of Christ that portrays an unconditional and unfailing love.
    - Though forged in adversity's fire, the caregiver's life goes from day to day, lending energy to console a loved one, but more importantly, being to them what God is to all of us: ***"an ever-present help in trouble"*** (Psalm 46:1).

- o Here lies the cornerstone for building a strong and intergenerational family. Here sounds the anthem that flows from the heart of God in His expressions of compassion. Here honor and love meet; the very honor and love that give dignity to the disabled and capture the value that God had already placed within them.

The Caregiver's Ethic: It's More Than about Me

- As the clock rolls and the calendar changes with the seasons, the unmet needs and constant demands mount, grinding at the caregiver's inner constitution. "God, what is expected of me? How much can I endure? Is there an end or even a reprieve? What about me?" In one instant, the wear and tear can erode at one's commitment.
- At another time the human spirit generates an inner strength that rises like a refiner's fire, purging the inner desires to gratify "self," and purifying one's ethic with an attitude that is other-oriented. But it is the clash in the inner man that wears with this intense continual challenge to one's ethic: Jesus' explicit expression that He came to serve (Mark 10:45).
- It was Jesus, who mastered bringing change by spending time among the weak and helpless. It is more than about me. In fact, "It's not about me, it's about others," was on continual display throughout his life and many of his early followers.

The Caregiver's Ethic: Its More Than about Me; It's about Others (Philippians 2:3-5)

"Do nothing out of selfish ambition or vain conceit, rather in humility value others above yourselves, not looking to your own interests but each of you to the interests of the others. In your relationships with one another, have the same mindset as Christ Jesus…"

- **Here stands the core of the Christian's ethic.**
  - o To place value upon others: It's more than about me. The truth is that it is about others.

The Caregiver's Rightful Title: Unsung Hero

- Caregivers, like all heroes, are willing to put everything at risk in order to save or assist a companion, drive back an enemy or achieve and hold a position that models courage and determination.

- No one signs up to be a hero. You earn it at the "intersection of happenstance and hell."
- Show me a hero, and I'll write you either a tragedy or story of true grit. Introduce me to a man of valor, and I'll introduce you to someone who has been on the front lines, who in a moment of time risked it all for something or someone else, because they held a deep-seated value that life is a gift to all.

Take-Away Thoughts
_____
_____
_____
_____

Caregivers...Study Guide

Homework - Session 2

1. **Read Chapter 3 – The Unsung Heroes** from *Caregivers: The Unsung Heroes of Our Day*. What additional thoughts or clarifications were helpful from the reading?

2. **Read Philippians 2:1-11**. This passage describes the core-ethic to Christianity and is expressed in the opening five verses.

    o What can you conclude that Paul meant when he states, "Do nothing out of selfish ambition or vain conceit. Rather, in humility value others above yourselves, not looking to your own interests but each of you to the interests of the others." (2:3-4)? What does it mean as a caregiver to "value others?"

    o If the Christian life sets as its core ethic that "life is more than about me" and asks of you to unselfishly express that kind of consideration for another, then what makes it so difficult to be a caregiver?

    o In Philippians 2:5-11, who is highlighted as the chief example of a servant?

- To what extent did Christ express his selfless attitude for you, and what bearing does this have on your thinking? What does this mean to you personally?

3. **Read Galatians 5:1, 13-26**
    - In Christ we are set free. What are you set free to do?

    - Who does the passage cite for you to lean upon to help you live?

    - What can we expect as a byproduct of this relationship?

**His love sets us free to serve.
True freedom finds expression in our care of others.**

Session 3: The Four Corners to Puzzling Events

Notes

Four Repeated Themes throughout the Scripture Pertaining to Adversity Lead Us to One Central Truth

❧ In this world, adversity comes to draw us to God and His likeness. ☙

How are we to understand and handle adversity?
What is at the heart of such difficult moments in life?

When a crisis (disability) hits, it...

It begins adversity's cycle that at any point draws us
Into harmony with the Almighty

1. Adversity awakens us to the hidden and painful side of life. (Genesis 3:7-10)
2. Adversity's challenges necessitate the need to make adjustments. (II Corinthians 1:8-11)
3. When a crisis hits, it ultimately transforms us. (II Corinthians 3:17-18; Romans 5:1-5)
4. Crises culminate in mobilizing us to action. (II Corinthians 1:3-4)

Take-Away Thoughts

_____
_____
_____

Homework - Session 3

1. **Read Chapter 4 – The Four Corners to Puzzling Events** from *Caregivers: The Unsung Heroes of Our Day*. What additional thoughts or clarifications were helpful from the reading?

2. Four repeated themes pertaining to adversity seem to appear and reappear throughout the Scriptures providing us with what we are calling the four corners to puzzling events. Making sense of how these concepts relate to each other and our own settings are what many of us have found helpful in framing our handling of adversity. **Take the time to think about each theme. Answer these questions:** Have you sensed these themes appearing? Do you find them repeating themselves or compounding, as the ill effects seem to multiply and create other hardships, in addition to the pains already encountered?

   Please keep in perspective that our remaining sessions will provide ample opportunity to address each point, but making a brief personal assessment can help establish a starting point for our journey in handling adversity. Respond briefly to each theme.

FOUR THEMES:

Corner Piece #1 - Adversity awakens us to the hidden and painful side of life. (Gen. 3:7-10)

Corner Piece #2 - Adversity's challenges necessitate the need to make adjustments. (II Corinthians 1:8-11)

Corner Piece #3 - When a crisis hits, it ultimately transforms us. (II Corinthians 3:17-18, Romans 5:1-5)

Corner Piece #4 - Crises culminate in mobilizing us to action. (II Corinthians 1:3-4)

3. It is noteworthy that these themes connect and reveal to us a cycle to understanding adversity. Understanding and having a frame of reference to handling our situation, and knowing where we are in adversity's cycle, helps us to more aptly process and respond to our circumstances, as well as interact with others about their present circumstances. As we shall see, it is important for anyone facing adversity to recognize the importance of living in the present tense and not buying tomorrow's projected complications. Take some time to think through the cycle of adversity and jot down initial thoughts that come to mind as you do.

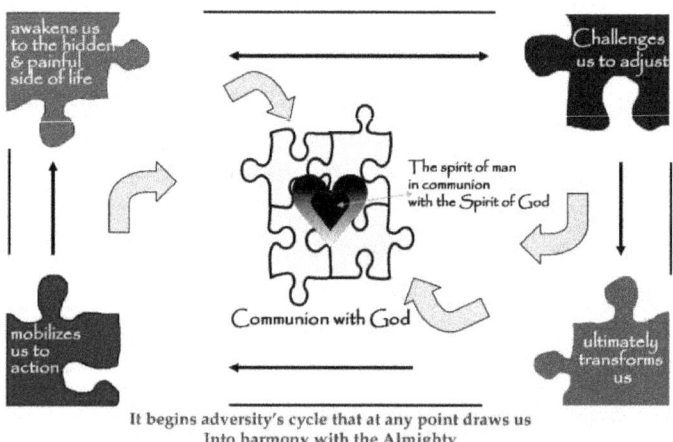

It begins adversity's cycle that at any point draws us
Into harmony with the Almighty

_____
_____
_____

So often many of us, in facing our adversity, merely react to our new circumstances the best we know how. Many times the tears have not even begun to dry up before we are thrust into action to offer assistance to a loved one. At the same time, we recognize that regardless of where we are in our journey, one central theme arises—*adversity comes to draw us to God.* State briefly your thoughts concerning this central theme pertaining to our relationship with God.

_____
_____
_____
_____
_____
_____

Session 4: Corner Piece # 1 (CP#1): When Crises Hit: Adversity's Immediate Effects & Handling the "Why, God?" Question

Notes
(This lesson contains a more extensive outline to allow us the opportunity to listen and to process what is being said in the class.)

☙ Crises awaken us to the immediate effects of adversity. ❧

Crisis Coping Skills – Broad Categories

- Marital satisfaction (if married) / family support;
    – Marital strain and family dysfunction only drains hope and drives us into despair
- Support group; Information from those in similar circumstances
- Peer mentors / Peer connection from someone who has handled a similar situation
- Social involvement / therapy, especially when it involves helping others, to get your mind off yourself. Here is where churches and local organizations can be real assets.
- Hobby dynamics: releases you from dwelling on hardship, especially if this hobby includes social involvement.
- Diet: Get into the mode of doing what is best for your nutrition, but, remember the monk's wise advice: "If I had to do it all over again, I would eat less beans and more ice cream."
- Natural enhancements: Dietary supplements to your diet
- Exercise: Proactive steps to help your body
- Moral and economic stability
- Counseling: Life assessment help that addresses such thoughts as "Woe is me, Life is horrible." Make the most of what I have; Life is a challenge.
- Faith: One's faith in God – notably prayer and one's view of God in crisis.
    – Life is God-given. Utilize what you have to live for Him.

Corner Piece #1:

Adversity Awakens Us to the Hidden and Painful Side of Life **Genesis 3:7, 10** "then the eyes of both of them were opened, and they realized they were naked; so they sewed fig leaves together and made coverings for themselves, [shame]… He answered, 'I heard you in the garden, and I was afraid because I was naked; so I hid.'"

Shame / covered / hid / blamed = alerted and alarmed

- **The Immediate Effects** That Accompany Crises
  - The lament Psalms – 6, 10, 13, 22, 46, 60, 142, etc. - "Why, God?"
- **Adverse Effects That Accompany Crises**

Immediate Effects

- Crises Awaken us to our own mortality
  A brush with death only stresses the fact that we are mortal beings

- Crises Awaken us to an Awareness of a Numinous Being
  o Who is the guardian to life and moral virtue?
  o Each person operates upon their own understanding of God, as they know Him at the moment
  o And then, there is the "Why, God?"

What does the word, "Why?" involve?

What underlying senses, emotions, and beliefs arise in the one word, "Why?"

  o Fear – Anxiety: surfaces in connection to the fact that matters at hand are out of control or unstable or, even worse, that life is uncertain or out of control.
  - Man lives with the illusion that he is in control.

  o Grief: overruns us because of the potential losses inflicted upon loved ones as well as ourselves. The "finality" associated with loss or death overcomes people, and death leaves devastating results and questions.

  o Confusion - Pointless Disbelief - Bewilderment / Shock

Every methodology has a pathology.

o Doubt – especially with God

"Why Lord?"

What does adding the word, "Lord," to the word, "Why?" imply?

- o **God is responsible.**
  If we reflect on the truth that His love is unfailing, and that evil in this world coexists with God, (due to sin) then the statement, "Why, Lord?" implies that God is responsible.

Yet, the question inadvertently expresses more an underlying statement directed at God, which leads us to be in faith, directing our heartfelt pains to the very One to whom we should turn in time of trouble. (Psalm 46)

In essence, "Why, God?" can be, and often is, more a statement of faith in God. It should be understood more as a reflective statement in His existence and relationship with us, even amidst the tears and confusion that often surround these settings.

- If we allow God to be God, He can answer when and as He sees fit, leading us to a better, more present tense question, which offers stability to us in crisis:

"How, Lord, would you have me respond?"

"Does God know? Has God allowed it to be? Then, God has a plan." (Derived from Gen.50:20)

- If we look at the occurrences of these words in the Scripture and see who was behind such words or similar sentiments, we can conclude that such questions are very fitting. For some of the godliest people the Scriptures have ever mentioned, in both Old and New Testament, have uttered them.
- Note that these words are a constant in the "Lament" Psalms of the Scripture. Psalms 6, 10, 13, 22, 46, 60 & 142 are examples in the Old Testament.

- Note the thoughts from the New Testament concerning the crises and the adversities that we face!
  - II Corinthians 1:3-11, 11, 12:1-10; Romans 5:1-11, 8:26-39; James 1:3-4; I Peter 1:3-9, 2:1-12, and 4:12-16.
  - John 16:33: "In this world you will have trouble, but take heart! I have overcome the world."
- The bottom line...*We, who find suffering at our door, are often numbered among some very godly company.*

Adversity Awakens Us to the Hidden and Painful Side of Life

- Crises Awaken us to the Fact that Something is Wrong with the World
  - There are forces greater than our capability to control
  - Sin has brought a curse to the world. Romans 8:20-22
- Crises Awaken us to the Fact that Something is Wrong with People
  - Man is a moral free will agent with legitimate longings & Man is sinful - Romans 3:23, 5:12
- Crises Awaken us to the Fact that Something is Wrong with Me
  - We are among the people and, therefore, just as much sinners.
- Crises Awaken us to Our Innate Longings (Next Session)
  - To a strength of human spirit to live: a fingerprint of God on mankind
- Crises Awaken us to Our Innate Longings – the fingerprints of God on mankind, if we choose to acknowledge them
  - He steps into our hardships to rescue and draw us to Himself.

Take-Away Thoughts
___
___
___

Homework - Session 4

1. **Read Chapter 5 – When Crises Hit** from *Caregivers: The Unsung Heroes of Our Day*. What additional thoughts or clarifications were helpful from the reading?

2. **Think through each of the immediate effects** brought on by adversity. Did any of these immediate effects occur in your situation and to what degree?

3. Lack of knowing how to address the "Why God?" question has led many people into a state of doubt about God. From the session and reading, what key points did you pick up to help you keep perspective in handling the immediate and even adverse effects of adversity?

4. How important is it to reach a point of understanding that, if God is God, then let Him answer the "Why, God?" question in His time, and let's focus upon answering the more important question of, "How Lord, would You have me to respond?"?

5. This world is not the way God created it to be. Sin and evil have distorted it, though all within the sovereign control and purpose of Almighty God. Crises reveal that we live in a broken world inhabited by broken people and rebellious spirits. The opening chapters to Job introduce us to a godly man who had adversity after adversity crash into his world. **Read the first three chapters.** One cannot help but ask, "How could this happen to such a godly man?" Addressing this question ultimately found Job face to face with God. **Read Job 38-42 and note specifically 42:1-6.** What can one conclude that Job came to understand, and which provided him the balance in handling his adversity?

Session 5: At the Heart of Adversity: Man in the Image of God

Understanding the coexistence of God and pain in adversity

Notes: This material is included in the session and workbook as a supplement to offer an explanation as to how God and pain co-exist in man, by exposing innate longings that, even with God present, can go unmet. "Thanks belong to Dr. Larry Crabb and his work *The Institute in Biblical Counseling* as well as his book *Marriage builder* in helping me form some of these ideas."

Man in the image of God: Genesis 1:26-28, 31

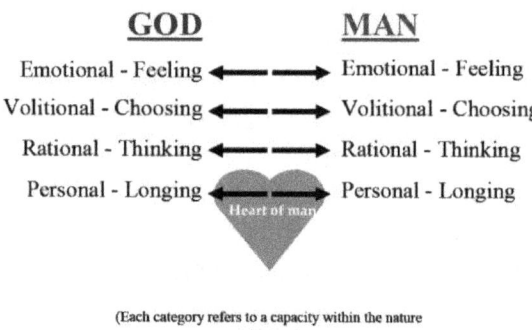

(Each category refers to a capacity within the nature of God and man)

Summarizing what we find:

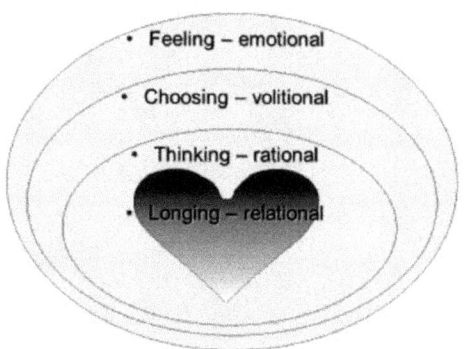

Image of God Reflected in Man

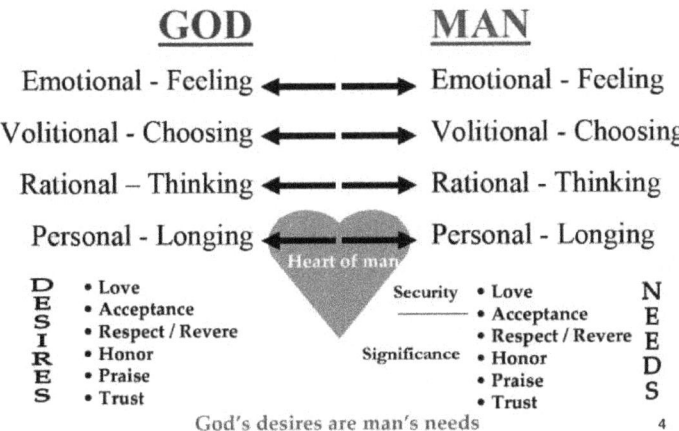

Security – love, relationship, identity, knowing that I belong
- A convinced awareness of knowing that I am loved without the need to change in order to win love; a love that is freely given by another, that was not earned and therefore, something one can rest, will not be lost.

Significance – impact, worth, knowing where I fit
- A realization that I am worthwhile and that I am engaged in a responsibility or cause, that is truly important. It entails one's

personal sense of value and purpose and the results of which will not evaporate with time, but leave a lasting legacy, even for eternity. This fundamentally involves having a meaningful impact on another person or influencing an honorable accomplishment and something for which I am adequate. **Which is dominant in the male and which in the female?**

The Heart of Man - Our Legitimate Longings
- **Distinction between soul and spirit**
- **Hebrews 4:12** - "For the word of God is living and active. Sharper than any double-edged sword, it penetrates even to *dividing soul and spirit*, joints and marrow; it judges the thoughts and attitudes of the heart."
- **Genesis 2:18** *The LORD God said,* "It is not good for the man to be alone. I will make a helper suitable for him."
    o Who is sitting next to Adam making the evaluation? What does this tell us?
    o God's evaluation – alone, incomplete
    o God's intention – a helpmate - one who brings completeness.
- **Soul:** the utilization of my capacities to relate, reason, choose and feel with people and my world
- **Spirit:** the utilization of my capacities to relate, reason, choose and feel with God

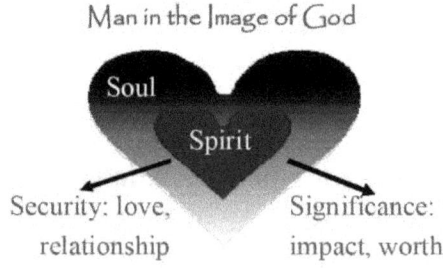

Man in the Image of God

Security: love, relationship

Significance: impact, worth

Caregivers...Study Guide

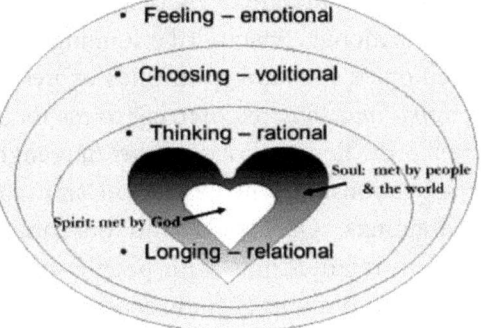

Take-Away Thoughts

_____
_____
_____

Homework - Session 5

The session unveiled an explanation as to the inner makeup of man with his capacities: emotionally, volitionally, rationally and relationally. It is noteworthy that in the relational capacity (the longings/needs of one's heart), the distinction between one's soul and spirit finds expression. Though writers will use both terms, *spirit and soul*, as referring to man's inner being, the fine line distinction occurs in the depth of one's heart in recognizing man's innate or inborn need for a relationship with both God and man are necessary to satisfy his deepest longings. Our souls find our quest for security and significance arising from relationships with people and the world in which we live. On the other hand, our spirits find security and significance coming from our personal relationship with Almighty God.

1. **Read the following sections for review: Page 69-72** in *Caregivers: The Unsung Heroes of Our Day*, which addresses the unmet legitimate needs, and **Pages 108-110** rehearses the material from Genesis 2 and the distinction of soul and spirit. Can you grasp the distinction between one's soul and one's spirit?

2. The intent of the lesson was to offer an explanation as to how God and pain co-exist in man by exposing the innate longings that, even with God present, can go unmet. For example, with God present, the experience of losing a valued loved one brings a mixed sense of security from God's presence, while the grief and tears flow from the loss. Can you identify through your time in the face of crisis where you could sense the awareness and comfort of God's presence while simultaneously hurting physically and emotionally in one's soul due to a legitimate need being unmet? Describe one setting where this was true.

Session 6: What Touches One Touches All: Adverse Effects on the Caregiver, the Family and Marriage & the Call to Encouragement

Notes:

Adversity Awakens Us to the Hidden and Painful Side of Life

Adverse Effects Facing Caregivers
~ Learning to Live in the Disabled Person's World
~ Heart-Wrenching Losses and Gut-Wrenching Anguish
~ Shattered Dreams and Exhaustion
~ False Guilt, Debilitating Grief, and Anxiety
~ Being Alone and Lonely
~ A Consuming Service within a Consuming Process
~ The Need for Help
~ The Need to Talk (Support Network)
~ Arriving Early to Old Age

Adverse Effects Facing Caregiver's Family
~ Impaired Family Activity, Peer Discrimination, and Hidden Fears
~ Awareness to an Unjust, Unfair World
~ Loss of Quality Time and Disrupted Role Function

Adverse Effects Facing Caregiver's Marriage
~ A Miscarriage of Marital Hope and Dreams, Leading to Depression and Bitterness
~ The Unmet Legitimate Needs Reserved for Marriage Alone: Companionship and Intimacy
~ The Hidden Personal Impairments: Economic Drain, Network Reduction, and Spiritual Disorientation

Corner Piece # 2 - Adversity's Challenges Necessitate the Need to Make Adjustments

Adjusting to being a caregiver...

1. Necessitates our embracing the commitment to care for the weak ~ Implies a call to encouragement

The Scriptures say...

- ~ Hebrews 3:13 "But encourage one another daily, as long as it is called, 'Today,' so that none of you may be hardened by sin's deceitfulness."
- ~ Hebrews 10:24-25 "And let us consider how we may spur one another on toward love and good deeds. [How?] Let us not give up meeting together, as some are in the habit of doing, but let us encourage one another..."
- ~ I Thessalonians 5:11 "Therefore encourage one another and build each other up, just as in fact you are doing."

Side 1: To Encourage = to strengthen (I Thessalonians 5:11, Hebrews 10:24-25)

- To put courage into someone
- To provide clarification and, therefore, affirmation
- To renew strength that has been lost or deadened
- To offer positive reinforcement

Side 2: To Comfort (II Corinthians 1:3-6)

- To provide consoling words or actions that communicates hope in the midst of loss or turmoil.
- He has an atmosphere about him that consoles the soul.

Side 3: To Exhort, to Correct and Get Them Back on Track. (Rom. 12:8, II Timothy 4:2)

- Here is the constructive conversation that empowers people to move on and not lose hope.
- This can be in an exhortative manner / correction or in a challenging sense

Side 4: To Be One's Advocate, To Support (I John 2:1)

- Here is the person who stands beside the one who is hurting and who comes to the defense of those who are weak.
- Here is the idea of reinforcement that expresses a value in the person being helped

The Fifth Side = the Inside - The Nature of Encouragement - A manifestation of the Trinity

- John 14:16-17; 25-26 - Who does Jesus refer to as the Counselor (NIV) or Helper?
  "…give you another Counselor to be with you forever – the Spirit of truth."
- II Corinthians 1:3-4 - Who does Paul refer to as the comforter?
  "Praise be to the God and Father…the God of all comfort who comforts us in all our troubles…"
- I John 2:1 (NASB) – Who does John refer to as the Advocate?
  "If anyone sins, we have an Advocate with the Father, Jesus Christ the righteous."

Why pick this word for the description of the Spirit, Father and Son?

The very nature of God radiates with Encouragement.

Biblical Encouragement:

To come alongside an individual (in a time of grief, needed guidance or a difficulty) and strengthen that person in a course of life, by causing him to look to the Lord and His Word for counsel.

Encouragement is meant to permeate the Christian's practice, because God's nature radiates with encouragement

Take-Away Thoughts

_____
_____
_____
_____
_____

Caregivers...Study Guide

Homework - Session 6

1. **Read Chapter 6 – At Least I Still Have Her** from *Caregivers: The Unsung Heroes of Our Day*. What additional thoughts or clarifications were helpful from the reading?

2. A Time to Reflect and Evaluate
   On a scale of one to ten, **evaluate how you think you have responded** to each of the adverse effects referred to in the book.
   - (1) refers to responding poorly and (10) means that you have responded very well.

   Learning to Live in the Disabled Person's World 1...2...3...4...5...6...7...8...9...10
   Heart-wrenching Losses & Gut-wrenching Anguish 1...2...3...4...5...6...7...8...9...10
   Shattered Dreams and Exhaustion 1...2...3...4...5...6...7...8...9...10
   False Guilt, Debilitating Grief and Anxiety 1...2...3...4...5...6...7...8...9...10
   Being Alone and Lonely 1...2...3...4...5...6...7...8...9...10
   A Consuming Service within a Consuming Process 1...2...3...4...5...6...7...8...9...10
   The Need for Help 1...2...3...4...5...6...7...8...9...10
   The Need to Talk 1...2...3...4...5...6...7...8...9...10
   Early Arrival to Old Age 1...2...3...4...5...6...7...8...9...10

   o **Which areas need your attention?** What one thing can you implement that will begin the process of improving this particular adverse effect?

3. **Read Chapter 7 - What Touches One Touches All** from *Caregivers: The Unsung Heroes of Our Day*. What additional thoughts or clarifications were helpful from the reading?

Personal Questions for Children

Take time to talk with each member of the family. You can use questions from below, which were some of the questions I asked my own family when they were grown looking back at the situation, or you can create your own that might better fit your setting. Remember to take into account their age levels, and choose words that they will understand.

1. From your viewpoint, how does the disability affect your disabled parent's relationship with you?
2. From your viewpoint, how does the disability affect your relationship with your caregiving parent?
3. How has your situation with a disabled family member affected your relationship to persons who are ...
   o physically disabled?
   o afflicted by chronic suffering? o people in general?
   o God?
4. How do you think your family has been hindered or hurt by the prolonged disability?
5. What could we as your parents do to help you adjust to the complications that have arisen due to this disability?
6. Have there been any benefits to our family as a result of this disability?
7. What would you like to know from your parents?
8. What advice would you offer to your parents to help you in your relationship with them?

Personal Questions for the Caregiver

Take time to contemplate each of the areas that affect your marriage and your place as a caregiver. Jot down your thoughts pertaining to each area.

1. What marital hopes and dreams have now become a part of your past? How have you responded to these losses?

2. Describe your relationship with your spouse at this moment in time. Articulate in writing your understanding of how this relationship provides a sense of security and significance for you.

3. On a scale of 0-10, with 10 being totally satisfied, rate the following. o How you view your intimacy factor:
    0...1...2...3...4...5...6...7...8...9...10
  o How you view your interaction with your spouse:
    0...1...2...3...4...5...6...7...8...9...10
  o How you view your enjoyment of each other's company:
    0...1...2...3...4...5...6...7...8...9...10

4. How has your situation affected the financial status of your home? Can you and your spouse interact about this area, or is it a point of contention?

5. What have you noticed about your circle of friends? In what way has being a caregiver affected your making and keeping friends?

NOTE: These questions have not been designed to offer solutions, as much of that will be addressed in the coming chapters. Yet, getting an honest assessment of your own situation is quite helpful and will prepare you for the next chapters.

Questions for Your Spouse

If you really feel bold, ask your spouse to respond to the same questions above that you have answered. This is purely voluntary, but let your spouse know that it is an exercise to help you understand your place as a caregiver.

1. What marital hopes and dreams have now become a part of your past? How have you responded to these losses?

2. Describe your relationship with your spouse at this moment in time. Articulate in writing your understanding of how this relationship provides a sense of security and significance for you.

3. On a scale of 0-10, with 10 being totally satisfied, rate the following. o How you view your intimacy factor:
    0…1…2…3…4…5…6…7…8…9…10
    o How you view your interaction with your spouse:
    0…1…2…3…4…5…6…7…8…9…10
    o How you view your enjoyment of each other's company:
    0…1…2…3…4…5…6…7…8…9…10

4. How has your situation affected the financial status of your home? Can you and your spouse interact about this area, or is it a point of contention?

5. What have you noticed about your circle of friends? In what way has the disability affected your making and keeping friends?

Session 7: Corner Piece # 2 (CP #2): Behind Closed Doors Part 1 - The Non-Negotiables of Caregiving

Notes

Corner Piece #2 – Adversity's Challenges Necessitate the Need to Make Adjustments to a New Normal.

1. **Necessitates our embracing the commitment to care for the weak:**
   - Adversity's effects translate into challenges that demand our attention.
     o We can't run. Whether we want to acknowledge it or not, we are involved.
   - Normalcy, as we knew it, is in question, and our family's security rests on the caregiver's shoulders.
   - We need to learn to live in the disabled person's world.
     o Medical needs, rehabilitative needs, personal, everyday needs
   - **Implies a call to encouragement**

Biblical Encouragement:

To come alongside an individual (in a time of grief, needed guidance or a difficulty) and strengthen that person in a course of life, by causing him to look to the Lord and His Word for counsel.

2. **Necessitates our willingness to redefine and reconstruct our lives: A new norm.**
   - **Implies an honest assessment of life, our purpose and our passion.**

   "I have learned to see every crisis as an opportunity for God to display Himself." Dawn Randall

   - Redefining life is a creative problem that begins by not allowing the losses to define our identity, but using the situation to reconstruct ourselves and our path of influence.

"The beauty of it is that this is a creative problem, not a follow-the-rulebook problem. You're not changing the oil. You're reinventing your life. You're a little messed up, sure, but you're also given a license to redefine yourself." Alan Rucker, *The Best Seat in the House*

Reconstruction Assessment

Think through the questions, making notes to your personal assessments.

1. What challenges and added responsibilities now confront your household? (Ex. Physical and medical needs, coordination of acute care and therapy visits, pharmaceutical and durable equipment needs, work adjustments, parental concerns, financial overload, etc.)

    Remember, added responsibilities tend to consume our time commitments, requiring us to adjust.

2. What responsibilities are essential to preserve for the overall well-being of the family? Are there needs within these that can be shifted to others to handle?

3. Accept that some of the normal family and personal activities must initially be put on hold through the adjustment phase of caregiving. What involvements or activities need to end or be temporarily set aside?

4. How will you need to adjust to meet the new challenges? What shifts in time schedules are necessary? Are there times during the week that can be left completely empty to provide opportunities to shift responsibilities to accommodate needs?

    A continued personal assessment is just as needed.

5. What have you established as your purpose for life? Has it been compromised by your circumstances? Have your new circumstances caused you to rethink your purpose? Take the needed time to think through and re-establish your purpose for your life and family. It can be amended, but knowing one's purpose has a way of giving direction, even on difficult days.

6. Some losses can be overwhelming. It is OK to shed tears. Tears are amazingly valuable for helping us cleanse our souls and provoke us to assess what is really valuable. Yet, make sure you remind yourself of what you have. (Ex. – I still have her.) What comes to mind that helps you maintain a healthy focus, as you fulfill all of your responsibilities?

7. What dreams and passions still reside within you that are being compromised? What must you put on the back burner or give up? Keep a diary of inner concerns and passions that surface in your thoughts. Are there recurring themes that require some time to address? Who is an available confidant with whom you can discuss this?

8. What necessary steps are needed to keep your health in check? This is essential for any caregiver.

Final thought from the Psalms

I. Overwhelming Problems: Psalm 13:1-2
A. The External Adversity & Silence of Heaven

> *V1 How long, O Lord? Will you <u>forget me forever</u>? How long will you <u>hide your face</u> from me?*

A day within the prison walls of adversity is much longer than a month in freedom's garden.

B. The Internal War
> *V2. How long must I wrestle with my thoughts and day after day have sorrow in my heart?*
>
> *How long will my enemy triumph over me?*

When God appears absent, evil seems near.

II. Triumphant Praise: Psalm 13:5-6

But I <u>trust</u> in your <u>unfailing love</u>; my heart rejoices in your salvation [deliverance] I will sing to the Lord, for He has been good to me.

How does he get from the overwhelming problems of 1-2 to the confident praise of 5-6?

III. Entrusting Prayer: Psalm 13:3-4

Look on me and answer, O Lord my God. Give light to my eyes, or I will sleep in death: my enemy will say, "I have overcome him," and my foes will rejoice when I fall.

Problems to Praise Pivot on Prayer.

The same prayer that pivots our problems to praise, acts as the hand of faith that translates promise into performance, and thereby refreshes and enlarges our view of the Lord.

Take-Away Thoughts

_____
_____
_____

Homework - Session 7

1. **Read Chapter 8** – "Behind Closed Doors from *Caregivers: The Unsung Heroes of Our Day*
   What additional thoughts or clarifications were helpful from the reading?

2. We have only looked at two of the non-negotiables to adjusting as a caregiver.
   - The first adjustment necessitates that we learn to embrace our commitment to care for the weak and implies that we become encouragers. Think it through on your own, making notes to yourself pertaining to areas that need your attention or improvement as an encourager. This is not a time to pass sentence on yourself, but it is a time to seriously and honestly make the necessary adjustments. Once you are done, speak to your spouse or a trusted friend about what you sense is needed.

   - The second adjustment necessitates our willingness to redefine and reconstruct our lives, which implies building a new normal. This requires an honest assessment of our lives, our purpose and our passion. Think through the reconstruction assessment offered in the session and further evaluate the thoughts and questions and what you could realistically start or accomplish.

One of the adjustments is to establish a purpose for yourself and your household.

A sample of one's purpose with God

Purpose: We are in this together
The Encompassing Purpose (Mandate) given by God: ***Live to the glory of God Or whatever you do, do it all to the glory of God*** (I Cor. 10:31b)

Implications: Everything you do should be done as if you're doing it for the Lord.

This implies that you know Him and want to make Him known as Paul would write, *"I want to know Christ and the power of his resurrection…"* (Philippians 3:10a)

Write out your purpose for your home. The Secret to this: Be "other-oriented." (Phil.2: 3-5) Join Christ in what He is doing.

Examples:
- Our purpose as a couple is to encourage families to follow Christ and mature in His likeness.
- We exist to honor and glorify God in all that we do and say.
- Our purpose as a couple is to encourage families to follow Christ, especially those who contend with the issues of disability and caregiving.

Specific Objectives (Process by which our purpose is fulfilled)
Once a purpose is established, it becomes essential to formulate a personal process to implement in order to accomplish His purpose for us.
- To multiply a godly heritage – In our own home and community
    "Our number one disciples live in our home."
- To mutually complete one's mate.
- To train (nurture) our children in the disciplines (character and skills) and admonitions of Christ (Eph. 6:3-4).
    o Disciplines – to instill the disciplines for life and the admonitions or instructions for life. Give them the moral reason "Why," to increase their understanding.
- Model Christ to our world.

Now, more specifically, how will we know if we have fulfilled our stated purpose? What would be reflected in our households and lives if our purpose is being fulfilled?

Product – Christ-like maturity is demonstrated in fully devoted followers of Christ. (Romans 8:28-29, Gal.4:19, Eph. 4:11-13)

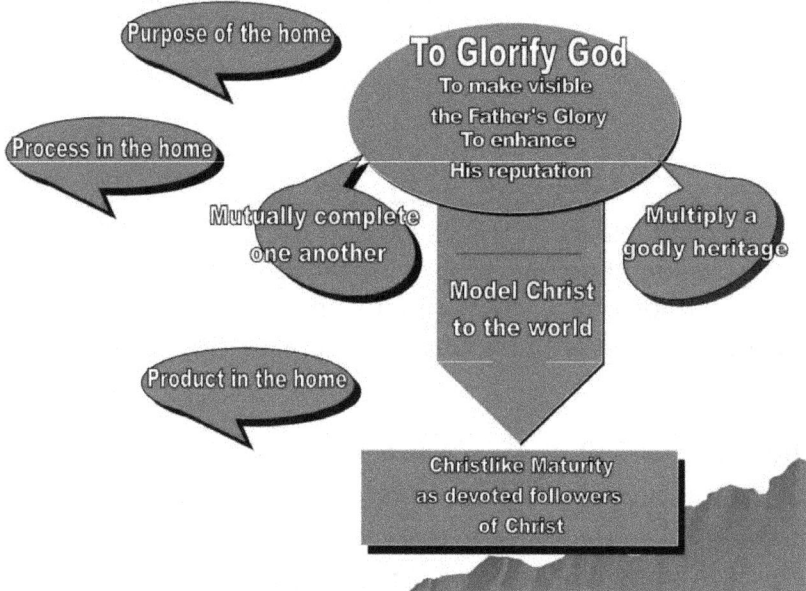

Session 8:
Corner Piece # 2 (CP#2): Behind Closed Doors
Part II - The Non-Negotiables of Caregiving

Notes

Corner Piece #2 - Adversity's challenges necessitate the need to make adjustments

Adjusting to being a caregiver...

1. Necessitates our embracing the commitment to care for the weak.
2. Necessitates our willingness to redefine and reconstruct our lives: A new norm.
3. **Necessitates the sensitivity to refine and nurture our own inner journeys.**
   ~ Implies a time to mourn and accept our calling to honor the Lord
     - Accept the challenge to re-prioritize our values pertaining to God, family and relationships; Talk about the future, and your relationship to God
     - Nurture a source of inner refreshment: Personal growth that addresses and focuses one's thoughts concerning God and how He would have us handle our setting is priceless. Establish a personal time, place and activity that aids this process of personal growth. Take time to pray.
     - Refine your Attitude: "It's not about me; it's about others."
     - Build a support network
     - Join a caregiver's support group
     - Be willing to ask and accept help; Even hire help
4. **Necessitates acknowledging the need to accept support, validation and even relief for ourselves, our disabled family member, and our family.**
   ~ Implies the need for a trusted confidant and support network
   ~ Implies the need to see that the family gets support
   ~ Implies individuality in parenting and developing healthy communication skills

- Establish a consistent family chat time (meals together)
- Provide individuality in parenting
- Give your family freedom to attend typical activities
- Provide creative family alternatives
- Set up a plan for family members to address personal concerns that arise in the home
- Take time to pray

5. **Necessitates our initiating invitations to new relationships and involvement in outside interests.**

Make new friends and keep the old; one is silver and one is gold.

- Be Hospitable: Plan to invite people into your home; take the initiative
- Invite new relationships
- Cherish meaningful relationships
- Foster trusted confidants (Even for children – grandma, adopted aunt/uncle)
- Be involved, look for ways to express compassion in service to others
- Maintain personal outside activity
- Join a small/support group (If possible, do it together)
- Find a healthy channel of personal refreshment; (coaching, etc.)
- Be a source of hope (personally, eternally)

Angels of Kindness – (Chapter 9 in Caregivers: The Unsung Heroes, is completely devoted to these extra special friends endowed with the precious gift of care.)

- An invitation to involvement
  o First Responders & the gift of "calm"
  o Angels – second class & the imprint of kindness o Fly-by angels
  o Extra Special Friends & the gift of "care"

If Christianity is anything, it is involvement. If community means anything, it means being willing to lift a hand to help someone in need. Love initiates action.

Kindness arrives as an outflow of God into our lives. Kindness can be summarized as a gesture of mercy by someone who takes a need into account and seeks to meet it. This is how God has seen and responded to believers, and it becomes a reflective quality of those who are followers of Him. In fact, where we lack, He supplies through the presence of His Holy Spirit, what is needed to communicate to those in need that He cares for them. We just happen to be the vessels of such kindness. What a privilege!

God's answers to prayer embolden our faith and strengthen us, as we await His response to those yet-unanswered requests.

Take-Away Thoughts

_____
_____
_____

Homework - Session 8

1. **Re-read Chapter 8 – Behind Closed Doors and then read Chapter 9 – Angels of Kindness** from *Caregivers: The Unsung Heroes of Our Day*. What additional thoughts or clarifications were helpful from the reading?

Adjusting to Being a Caregiver…
- o Necessitates our embracing the commitment to care for the weak, And it implies the need to be an encourager.
- o Necessitates our willingness to redefine and reconstruct our lives, And implies an honest assessment of our lives, our purpose and our passion.
- o Necessitates the sensitivity to refine and nurture our own inner journeys, And implies a time to mourn and accept our calling to honor the Lord.
- o Necessitates acknowledging the need to accept support, validation, and even relief for ourselves, our disabled family member, and our family, And implies the need for a trusted confidant and support network, the need to see that the family gets support, and the need for individuality in parenting and developing healthy communication skills.
- o Necessitates our initiating invitations to new relationships and involvement in outside interests.

2. **Take each of the above necessary adjustments and assess yourself.** Are there areas of adjustment that need to be addressed? Think it through on your own, making notes to yourself pertaining to areas that need your attention. Again, this is not a time to pass sentence on yourself, but a time to seriously and honestly make the necessary adjustments. Once you are done, speak to your spouse or a trusted friend about what you sense is needed.

   o **Which of the five** do you consider you have made the quickest adjustment to, and what makes you conclude this?

   o **Which of the five** do you consider the one needing the most of your immediate attention, and who can you discuss this with to help hold you accountable to attain that adjustment? **Explain what compels you** to note this area as needing your attention.

   o **Name some angels of kindness** to your household. **If possible, express in a note or word** a "Thank you," for being an "Angel in disguise."

Session 9: In Sickness and in Health: Best Friends by God's Design

Notes

God's Masterpiece in Creation - Genesis 1:26-28, 31
- In the act of creation, the priority social relationship for all society was fixed as that of a man to a woman, husband to wife. (Couch Time)
- God's dream in creation culminates in a masterpiece, featuring a man and woman in relationship with God and with each other.

Marriage is a dream within a dream: Our dream within God's. Genesis 1:31 "It is very good."

God's Master Plan - Genesis 2:18-23
The LORD God said, "It is not good for the man to be <u>alone.</u> I will make a <u>helper</u> suitable for him."

- God's evaluation – state of being alone or more incomplete.
  - Was Adam alone? Who was there?
- God's intention - helpmate: one who brings completeness.
  o Who is sitting next to Adam making the evaluation?
  o The word "helpmate" is the same word used of God in Ps 46:1 "My very present help in trouble."
  o God's intention was to create woman, who would be to man in his soul what God Himself already was in His spirit: *One who brought completeness.*

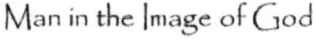

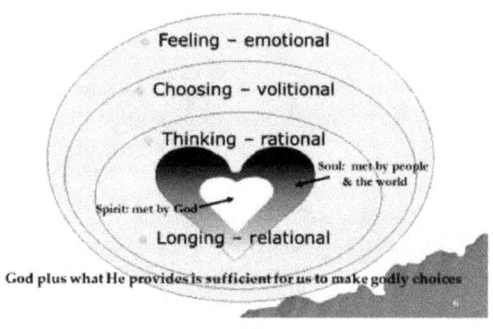

The words soul and spirit are words that are often used to capture the idea of what is referred to as the inner, unseen part of man. Poets often used these words synonymously and in doing so almost leave the impression they are one in the same. The writer of Hebrews though challenges our thinking mind when he writes, "For the word of God is living and active. Shaper than any double-edged sword, it penetrates even to dividing soul and spirit, joints and marrow: it judges the thoughts and attitudes of the heart." (Hebrews 4:12).

This passage leads us to understand that the Scriptures detect that the words soul and spirit are distinct words with distinct meanings that the Scriptures see as separate and different. In other words, these two words refer to two distinct intricate parts of the nature of mankind. Let's be careful though in that the words are both used at times referring to the inner man.

Understanding man in the image of God has given us a picture of man's inner capacities. (See diagram Man in the Image of God above). Uniquely the opening chapters to Genesis also provide a beautiful uncovering of man's heart, as seen in Adam, finding fulfillment with both God and another of his own kind, namely Eve. It is here that the ideas of one's spirit and soul find expression.

The spirit of a human being refers to the inner, unseen, make-up of both men and women alike that finds them utilizing the four inner capacities to relate, to think, to choose and to feel in response to one's relationship with God. Distinctly different than the rest of creation, the core of man's heart with its distinct longings or needs for security and significance finds fulfillment only in a relationship with God. In short, every human being has within them longings that are reserved for only God and the love and meaningful significance that fills man's heart through that relationship with God, alone. Without a personal encounter and relationship with God Himself, the void and emptiness within the man's spirit for his deepest longings of security and significance, go unmet.

At the same time **the soul** of any human being refers to the inner, unseen, make-up of both men and women alike that finds them utilizing the four inner capacities to relate, to think, to choose and to feel in response to one's relationship with people and their world. Where the heart shaped vacuum of man's spirit seeks a relationship with God, the soul with its same need for security and significance finds fulfillment through relationships with others of their own kind and through one's involvement in meaningful impact in one's world.

Caregivers...Study Guide

- **While You Were Sleeping: Gen. 2:19-21 – God was at work**

"So the Lord God caused the man to fall into a deep sleep; and while he was sleeping, he took one of the man's ribs and closed up the place with flesh." (v21)

- **The Master's Plan: Gen. 2:22-23 - Mutual completeness.**

"Then the Lord God made a woman from the rib he had taken out of the man, and he brought her to the man. The man said, 'This is now bone of my bones and flesh of my flesh; she shall be called "woman," for she was taken out of man.'"

Moses' Commentary on the Creation Account - Genesis 2:24-25

"<u>For this reason</u> a man will <u>leave</u> his father and mother and be united (<u>cleave</u>) to his wife, and they will <u>become one</u> flesh. The man and his wife were <u>both naked</u>, and they felt no shame."

God's Master Plan - *"For this reason"*
- Mutual completeness: Entails both the man and the woman in relationship with each other and the Creator Himself, and involves four timeless qualities:

Four Timeless Qualities

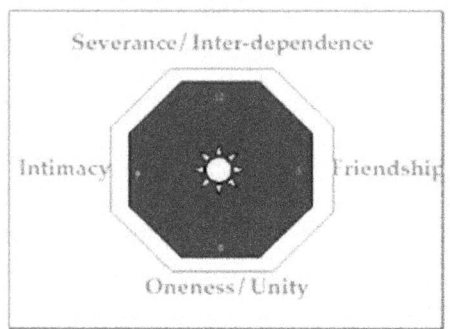

of a hallmark Marriage

50

The Biblical Premise to a hallmark Marriage: Friendship: "Cleaving to his Wife"

- **Unite – cleave - dabaq (daw-bak') קבד - to cleave to, to cling, to stick, to paste or be glued together, to permanently bond together.** o In relational contexts: to cling in affection and loyalty, to hold onto with both hands. It is used as the action verb or activity between those who are close friends, the closest of friends being one's spouse (Proverbs 18:22, 24).
o Permanence in the context of friendship means, *"I will be there."* o It is used in relationships to depict a friendship.

In the context of a marriage, unity and intimacy are by-products of the cleaving or being best friends.

- **My darling - Endearment – rayah (ra-yah) היער – companion, beloved, my love, my darling - Song of Solomon 1:9, 15; 2:2, 10, 12**
o It means to be associated, a friend, a guard, comrade, companion and close associate
o It is a derivative of the word, "to shepherd" or to be one who cares for another. (S. of S. 1:7)
o In intimate expressions, it means *"my darling."*

- **Love their husbands – philandrous (phil-androus) φιλανδρους, love their husbands.**
o **A derivative from the word "Phileo" - Love – Titus 2:3-5** *"Likewise, teach the older women...to teach what is good. Then they can train the younger women to love their husbands* (**philandrous**)*..."* o **"phileo"** – φιλέο – is one of the Greek words for love. It is word that is translated by the word friend or brotherly love. It implies a comradeship, a mutual sharing of thoughts, dreams, plans and attitudes that would be shared with no one else.
o It implies trust and confidence in another, leaving us with the understanding that a friend is a "trusted confidant."

A Friend: A trusted confidant - Friendship is a trust relationship between two people who are mutually drawn to each other. Their unselfish concern, respect, and tenderness influence them to draw closer to each other and to God, in whom real meaning is found.

Caregivers...Study Guide

Vital Characteristics of a Friend

Vital Characteristic of a Hallmark Marriage:

- **Loyalty:** A sentimental devotion marked by faithfulness and reliability: Not a sometimes love *"A friend loves at all times"* – Prov. 17:17
- **Enjoyment / Laughter / Having fun together**

    "A cheerful heart is good medicine" – Prov. 17:22
    Friendship enables you to "dance" in spite of your differences.

- **Sharing Deeply:** Embracing each other's thoughts, dreams, feelings, attitudes and passions. It is here that the vault to one's heart is opened.

    "Love is a four letter word spelled T-I-M-E."

- **Sacrifice: Kindness and Service** – Giving of yourself for your spouse.

    A servant's motto: "How can I help you?" (Ruth 2:8-18 coupled to Philippians 2:3-8)
    The best place to find a helping hand is at the end of your arm.

- **Encouragement:** Coming alongside to strengthen or reinforce your spouse in the course of life. (Hebrews 3:13, 10:24-25)

  The very nature of God radiates with encouragement.

- **Stimulation:** Challenging each other to reach new horizons (Hebrews 10:24-25)

  The interaction and exchange of insights to life
  Expanding one's focus, thoughts and insights: *"What do you think?"*

- **Purpose – Synergy:** We are in this together.

  The Encompassing Purpose (Mandate) given by God:
  Live to the glory of God
  - (I Cor. 10:31)

"Whatever else may be said about the home, it is the bottom line of life,
the anvil upon which attitudes and convictions are hammered out.
It is the place where life's bills come due,
the single most influential force in our earthly existence.
No price tag can adequately reflect its value.
No gauge can measure its ultimate influence…for good or for ill.
It is at home, among family members that we come
to terms with circumstances.
It is here that life makes up its mind."
C. Swindoll

Take-Away Thoughts

_____
_____
_____
_____
_____
_____

Homework - Session 9

1. **Read Chapter 10** Best Friends by God's Design from *Caregivers: The Unsung Heroes of Our Day*. What additional thoughts or clarifications were helpful from the reading?

2. **Couch time – 15 minutes**
   - Find a favorite spot to talk with each other while you share your favorite dessert. This time is meant to highlight that the priority social relationship is that of husband and wife. The ground rules for these 15 / 20 minutes involve a couple sitting together enjoying dessert and conversing. Yet in this conversation you are not allowed to talk about work, money or family. Kids can be kept busy and are not to interrupt (unless there is an absolute emergency, which means there is blood).
   - Remember, a best friend can be defined as one who is a "trusted confidant, to whom one is drawn." To be best friends is to have a hallmark marriage, just as God designed, with Him at the center of that relationship.
   - To get you started in the enrichment process of your friendship, individually write down and then discuss your definition of a friend. Take the time to interact and reach a working definition that both of you can agree to. The next question involves writing down the qualities that you would consider as qualities that make a best friend a best friend. As you eat dessert together, offer your understanding and tell why you put such value on the qualities of friendship that you chose.

3. We took time in the class to look briefly at the component parts of a friendship. **Now, take the time to rate your relationship on a scale of 1-10** with 10 being excellent. How are you doing in each area? Interact as a couple, as to your evaluation.

Loyalty 1....2....3....4....5....6....7....8....9....10

Enjoyment 1....2....3....4....5....6....7....8....9....10

Sharing Deeply   1....2....3....4....5....6....7....8....9....10

Sacrifice   1....2....3....4....5....6....7....8....9....10

Encouragement   1....2....3....4....5....6....7....8....9....10

Stimulation   1....2....3....4....5....6....7....8....9....10

Purpose   1....2....3....4....5....6....7....8....9....10

4. **Be prepared to share with the group**. Remember this is a support group, and we are here to help each other. Nothing to hide!!
5. **During Couch Time this week compare your answers** and have fun interacting with the following questions as you do:

    o Which of these characteristics do you find as strengths within your relationship?

- In which of these qualities are you strong as an individual? How can this help both of you in enriching your friendship?

- Are there any characteristics that you find yourselves as being opposites? How does this demonstrate itself in your relationship?

- In which areas have you found that you are both weak? Determine one way to strengthen this characteristic. Jot down your conclusion.

- Together conclude on one practical lesson that you can implement to enrich the friendship factor in your marriage.

6. **Write out your purpose for your home**. We had you do this is session
7. Has much changed or has the idea of your purpose been overlooked?

   Review, and if necessary, revise your purpose which basically answers the question what are we doing together as a couple? What are we as a couple seeking to accomplish together?
   - The secret to this: Be "other-oriented" (Phil.2: 3-5). Join Christ in what He is doing.

Session 10: Corner Piece # 3 (CP#3): The Fingerprints of God

Constructive Transformation & Keeping Perspective When Life Stings

- Strength of Human Spirit
- Transforming Acceptance
- Power of the Powerless

"God's fingerprints are all over Adversity, but probably not the way we would think."

Notes

A Brief Review:

How are we to understand and handle adversity?
What is at the heart of such difficult moments in life?

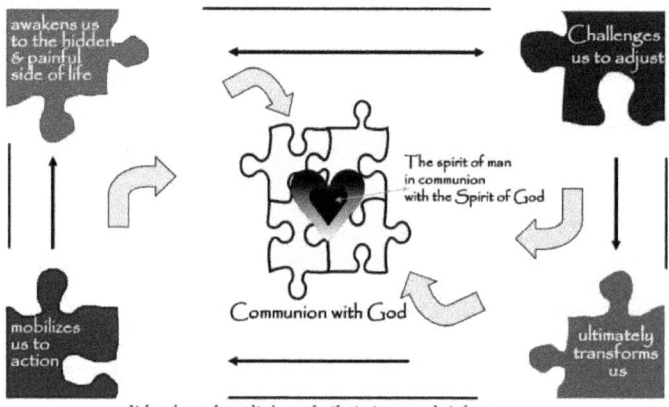

When a crisis (disability) hits, it...
- awakens us to the hidden & painful side of life
- Challenges us to adjust
- mobilizes us to action
- ultimately transforms us

The spirit of man in communion with the Spirit of God

Communion with God

It begins adversity's cycle that at any point draws us Into harmony with the Almighty

Corner Piece # 3: How do we handle when a crisis hits?
- When a crisis (disability) hits, it ultimately **transforms us.**
  o **Transformation,** different than **change,** implies that something acts upon us.
- **II Cor. 3: 18** "…And we, who with unveiled faces all reflect the Lord's glory, are being transformed into his likeness with every-increasing glory, which comes from the Lord, who is the Spirit."
- **Romans 8:28-29** "And we know that in all things God works for the good of those who love him, who have been called according to his purpose. For those God foreknew he also predestined to be conformed to the likeness of his Son…"
- **Romans 5:1-5** "Therefore, since we have been justified through faith, we have peace with God through our Lord Jesus Christ, through whom we have gained access by faith into this grace in which we now stand. And we rejoice in the hope of the glory of God. Not only so, but we also rejoice in our sufferings, because we know that suffering produces perseverance; perseverance, character; and character, hope. [*it is a process*]. And hope does not disappoint us, because God has poured out his love into our hearts by the Holy Spirit, whom he has given us."

Fingerprints of God on Humanity: Seeing them, requires knowing what to look for.

1. **Strength of Human Spirit: a dynamic woven into the fabric of humanity; an innate quest to live**

    "It overcomes vast hurdles but needs to be loved and nourished."
    Jill Krementz, *How It Feels to Live with a Disability* p.9

"You have more emotional grit, more resolve, and greater perseverance than you imagine. Let me be the first to tell you, you are not the weak sister you think you are… I don't know where so many people get the idea that they don't have what it takes to bear up under such stress… Maybe, many of us have had so little true stress in our lives that it looms as more unbearable than it often is. The 'catastrophizing,' in other words, is worse than the catastrophe, or maybe it is just human nature to fear the unknown."

Alan Rucker, *Best Seat in the House*

- Where does this inner drive to live come from?
- Why does this innate resolve surface, especially in the face of adversity, to empower a person to expend his all, when his life is in question?
- How is it that, even the great accuser before God (in Job's story) would conclude that, "man will give all he has for his own life"?
- How is it that regardless of nationality, race or sex, man, woman and child seek, in death's face, to live and fight for life?

Fingerprint of God on Humanity: Strength of Human Spirit
- God's fingerprint on the human soul has provided every human being with an intrinsic quest for life. This innate drive to live stems from mankind's first breath, which was breathed into man by God himself.

> ***"God formed the man from the dust of the ground and breathed into his nostrils the breath of life, and the man became a living being"***
> (Genesis 2:7).

- God gave life with the full intent of having man live life and do so in harmony with Him.
- God's fingerprint on the soul carries a "DNA for life," reflected in man's desire to live.

Fingerprint of God on Humanity: Transforming Acceptance

2. **Transforming Acceptance: takes the already-defined challenges, acknowledges them as they are, and receives them as they are offered.**

   "Adversities are nothing more than great opportunities for God to display Himself. Dawn, see your disability as an opportunity for the Lord."
   Winnie C. - Missionary with Oversees Missionary Fellowship

   "Acceptance blows the lights out on the pity party, which is no big loss."

- **Acceptance initiates transformation and creates a perseverance that makes change possible.**
  - Acceptance initiates transformation. Why shouldn't it? Think about it!!
  - Acceptance implies a complete honesty with the situation. "Nothing escapes you, O Lord."
  - Honesty is the core to humility. **(Romans 12:3)** For humans we typically think more highly of ourselves, which is what we refer to as pride or we think more lowly of ourselves, which is what is referred to as "false humility."
  - He gives grace to the humble. (I Peter 5:5) – to those who are honest with themselves and with God Almighty.
  - Grace awakens gratitude, and gratitude awakens commitment and the needed perseverance for change.
- Having adjusted to the adverse effects brought on us by adversity, the quality of acceptance opens the doorway to the transforming ways of Almighty God. It is here that we make a choice that, working with God's transforming ways, brings the changes to our character, values, motives and understanding, often times without us being conscious of the actions of God. Here is where we are ultimately transformed by our adversity.
- This is just as true in the non-Christian as it is in the Christian.

Corner Piece # 3 - Fingerprints of God on Humanity

1. **Strength of Human Spirit**
2. **Transforming Acceptance: takes the already-defined challenges, acknowledges them as they are, and receives them as they are offered.**
3. **Power of the Powerless**

"Feeding Oliver throughout his life was like feeding an
eight-month old child...
Though we breathed the same night air, listened to the same wind, slowly
without our knowing, Oliver created a certain power around us,
which changed all our lives.

I cannot explain Oliver's influence except to say that the powerless in our world do hold great power. The weak do confound the mighty." C. de Vinck, ***The Power of the Powerless***

"The Power of the Powerless breaks with all human logic, all intelligent predictions, all normal norms of success and satisfaction. It turns everything upside down.
It speaks not only about the power of the powerless, but also about love offered by those who cannot speak words of love, joy by those who suffer grievously, hope given by those whose lives are complete failures, courage enkindled by those who cannot make the slightest move on their own. In a world that so much wants to control life and decides what is good, healthy, important, valuable and worthwhile, they will find that the hidden truths of life are hidden from the learned and clever and revealed to those who are mere children (Mt 11:25)."
Henry Nouwen, in ***The Power of the Powerless***, C. de Vinck

"If Oliver had not been born
I would not have the same joys and fears and secrets I dream about today...
There was a substance in the house beyond science and philosophy and theology, for these are man-made explanations."
C. de Vinck,

- **The Drawing Salve of Almighty God**

"My grace is sufficient for you, for my power is made perfect in weakness"
II Corinthians 12: 9

His power is more like a drawing salve that pulls out of people.

"Now the Lord is the Spirit, and where the Spirit of the Lord is, there is freedom.
And we, who with unveiled faces all reflect the Lord's glory, are being transformed into his likeness with ever-increasing glory, which comes from the Lord, who is the Spirit"
(II Cor. 3:17-18).

In a crisis opportunity knocks with a gentle reminder that all there is of God is available to the man who is available to all there is of God.

Constructive Transformation within Crises

- Formation of a spirit compassion and empathy (II Cor. 12:9-10)

    These qualities, along with forgiveness, require pain and or evil to see them displayed. These serve as God's undeniable qualities in a perishing world marred by sin. Here God exposed Himself and His being like never before in eternity.

- Encouragement to place value on others - Phil 2:1-5
- Refinement of faith - Romans 5:1-5

Hang around the disabled, those in chronic pain or suffering, or the ill or terminally ill, and your life will undoubtedly change.

Keeping Perspective "When Life Stings"

Take-Away Thoughts

_____
_____
_____

Homework - Session 10

1. **Read Chapter 11 The Fingerprints of God** from *Caregivers: The Unsung Heroes of Our Day*. What additional thoughts or clarifications were helpful from the reading?

    This session focuses upon "The Fingerprints of God," which involves recognizing a transforming action on God's part upon those who find themselves accepting and owning their situation as caregivers. The concept of a fingerprint may seem foreign to the idea of God, but if we can see what is being said more as a metaphor of expressing God's involvement rather than His actual fingerprints, the ideas here can serve to enhance our awareness of the process of handling adversity.

    Fingerprints are often not seen unless one has the right dusting powder that can be spread over the scene. Here the Scriptures serve as that "dusting powder," revealing certain hidden "fingerprints" of God. In this lesson three of God's fingerprints were revealed: the strength of human spirit that has been planted in all mankind, the transforming power of acceptance, and, lastly, the power resident within the powerless and which ultimately then transforms all who come under its influence.

Strength of Human Spirit

2. **Look back at your time as a caregiver**. Describe a situation from your own setting that exemplifies the unique strength of the human spirit to rise up against the complexities brought on by the hardship that has gripped your household.

Transforming Acceptance

3. We have already seen that when a crisis hits, it ultimately transforms us (II Corinthians 3:17-18, Romans 5:1-5). Yet in this transformation process Paul reached a point of acceptance with what he referred to in one situation as his "thorn in the flesh." This acceptance implies a complete honesty with his situation. Even though he felt he could do so much more if his thorn was removed, **read II Corinthians 12:7-10** to find what the Lord impressed upon Paul and all of us, as we find ourselves relying on our own self- sufficiency. **Can you reflect upon an incident or moment that displays His fingerprint of how acceptance has transformed your life?**

Power of the Powerless

4. **Read II Corinthians 12:1-10**. Recognize that the person whom Paul knew who had seen visions (12:1-7) was probably himself. Whether it was or not, Paul alludes to the fact that because of these revelations he was given a "thorn in his flesh" as he was definitely privy to the information. Much speculation has arisen as to the exact nature of this "thorn", but from Paul's own words it came to keep him from becoming conceited, (12:7). Another way of looking at this idea of conceit is to recognize it as another way of dealing what we refer to as being a little "self-righteous." Maybe the "thorn" came in addressing the self-righteous manner that he displayed. Once his self-righteous manner was dealt with over those 14 years, Paul again asked the Lord on three occasions to remove the thorn. In our contemporary way, it would be like us saying, "What would be the point? Remove this thorn so I could really be free to be about your business, Lord!" To this point of being self-sufficient, God then responds and as the passage then unfolds, a third of God's fingerprints, namely the "power of the powerless", goes to work. Here the power finds expression, not so much as explosive, but as a drawing salve upon all in its reach. As a caregiver, note how your life has been affected. **What noticeable changes do you find within yourself that you know have come**

from your calling as a caregiver?

5. **Read Romans 8:28-29** If God's desire for us involves our becoming conformed into the likeness or image of His Son, what can we conclude when we find changes that make us more sensitive, compassionate, kind, willing to help and care for the needy?

6. Read **Chapter 12 Where Noble Dreams Are Born from** *Caregivers: The Unsung Heroes of Our Day.* What additional thoughts were helpful from the reading?

- **Respond to the conclusion in the chapter** that leaves us with a key thought that...

It is in the crucible of personal pain and suffering that the noblest dreams are born, And the God-given passions are conceived in compensation for what one has patiently endured. (Derived from thoughts from Psalm 90:15 and a quote by Whitney Phipps.)

- As a caregiver or one who faces a chronic condition, what one noble dream has been born, or personal passion conceived, along your journey? If none at this moment, then recognize that, as we patiently endure, we need to be open to possibilities. Also do not overlook the possibility of joining, serving in, or initiating a Support Group, yourself.

Session 11: Corner Piece #4 (CP#4):
Let's Make Music: Mobilized to Action

Notes

How are we to understand and handle adversity?
What is at the heart of such difficult moments in life?

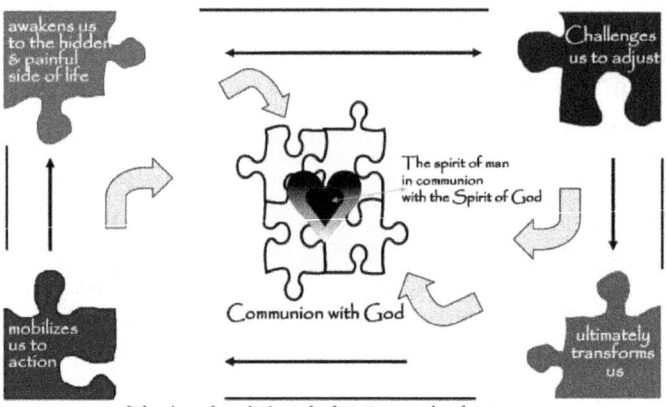

It begins adversity's cycle that at any point draws us
Into harmony with the Almighty

Corner Piece #4 - Crises culminate in mobilizing us to action

**It is in the crucible of personal suffering that the noblest
dreams are born, And the God given passions are conceived
in compensation for what one has patiently endured.**
Derived from thoughts from Psalm 90:15 and a quote by Whitney Phipps.

**Motivated by Grace and Compelled by Love: Gratitude
awakens commitment.**

- **God's Delight: Exercising His unfailing love for those in need**
    - The Scriptures say that at the heart of God's own desires lies His delight in displaying lovingkindness.

        > "I am the Lord, who exercises kindness,
        > justice and righteousness on earth, for in
        > these I delight" (Jeremiah 9: 24).

    - Some translators use the **idea of mercy** for lovingkindness, (… do justice, love <u>mercy</u>, as in Micah 6:8 NIV) while still others find the Old Testament word, (חסד– hesed) better expressed by the words **unfailing-love or kindness**.
    - Whichever the choice, one truth cannot be missed: **this word captures the very nature of God.**

He delights in exercising His unfailing love – loving-kindness – His mercy for those in need.

This act of unfailing love or mercy toward one in need is referred to as an act of grace.

- **Awakened to the Meaning of God's Grace -The Attitude of Gratitude**
    - The word for grace, in Greek, is **charis (χάρις),** which means *the unmerited favor of one to another.*
    - When we realize that grace is a gift, we then understand why the Romans used the word, *grata*, to translate the word, *charis*. It is from the word, **grata**, that we get our word, **gratitude**.
    - Inherent in the understanding of grace is the intrinsic or inner sense of gratitude that is awakened. Therefore, when grace is understood it awakens gratitude, and **gratitude then awakens commitment**.
    - This is **the primary and most unstoppable form of motivation,** for it is **intrinsic** and **focused completely and solely upon one's relationship with Christ.**

Awakened to the Meaning of God's Grace
-The Attitude of Gratitude-
I Corinthians 15:1-10

Unmerited act of love as a gift

Divine enablement
That accompanies
His Presence

Internal, intrinsic, Gratitude
that is awakened
to empower the heart
of man

Grace empowers each of us to live as God intended man to live:
Like Christ

- **Awakened to the Meaning of God's Grace: The Attitude of Gratitude**

    o It is also why Paul could say what he did in I Corinthians 15:10: "But by the grace of God I am what I am, and his grace to me was not without effect. No, I worked harder than all of them—yet not I, but the grace of God that was with me."

    o Paul was who he was because of God's unmerited love or grace. He labored all the more, but not because he was trying to earn points with God. It was his overwhelming sense of gratitude, awakened by his awareness of God's gift, that empowered his commitment to serve Christ.

    o Try to stop a man like that! In Paul's case, this empowered him to accomplish so much more for the sake of Christ.

The Attitude of Gratitude

> **The grace of God cost everything for the giver and nothing for the recipient.**
> It is love that stooped to bring the best to man, free of charge.
> Grace means that there is nothing more that we can do
> to make God love us more, and there is nothing more that we can do
> to make God love us less. Grace already loves as much
> as any infinite God can possibly love.

Caregivers...Study Guide

The Heartbeat of Caregivers

The Pathway to Friendship with God: Shipwreck your ego.

Man's Dilemma: Man's plight because of sin

1. How do I gain a righteous position before God Almighty?
   What is necessary for me to be declared as righteous "in His sight?" Romans 3:19-30
2. What is the remedy to the consequences brought upon myself because of my own sinfulness?
   What is necessary to satisfy His justice, remove the curse of separation from God & restore man to a relationship with the Lord?
3. How do I overcome this temporal enslavement to sin's power?
   What is necessary to empower man to overcome his innate impulses which enslave him to his own sin nature?
   How do I keep short accounts?

Friendship with God and another,
committed to the same but higher purpose.

Caregivers...Study Guide

The Nature of Sin

Man's Depravity

Can man do good enough to merit standing as acceptable before a Holy God or justified in God's sight?

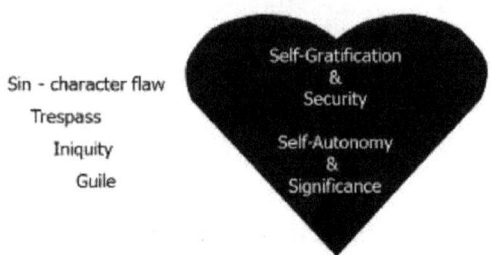

Sin - character flaw
Trespass
Iniquity
Guile

Self-Gratification & Security
Self-Autonomy & Significance

Romans 3:20 *"Therefore no one will be declared righteous In His sight by observing the law; rather, through the law we Become conscious of sin."*

Preach the Gospel to Yourself

- **Remember the Cross: Christ's Atoning Work** - Romans 3:9-31

    The gospel of Jesus Christ takes into account that... o It is God's Law that Christ perfectly obeyed.
    o It is God's love that Christ expressed. o
    It is God's wrath that Christ exhausted.
    o It is God's justice that Christ satisfied by dying for
    us. o From God's presence, Christ removed our sins.
    o From God's curse, which separated us from God, Christ redeemed us.
    o Into God's divine presence, He reconciled us.

- **Rehearse our forgiveness:** Colossians 1:14; Romans 8:1-2

    o "in whom (the Son) we have redemption, the forgiveness of sins." (Col. 1:14)
    o "Therefore, there is now no condemnation for those who are in Christ Jesus, because through Christ Jesus the law of the Spirit of life set me free from the law of sin and death." (Rom 8:1-2)
    o Luke 7: 47 Gratitude awakens commitment: "...her many sins have been forgiven – for she loved much. But he who has been forgiven little loves little."

Caregivers...Study Guide

Understand the accumulated indebtedness that Christ forgave.

- **Grace that Gives - Philippians 2:1-8**
  o Eliminates selfish ambition
  "…consider others better than yourselves": place value on others "Look not only to your own interests (responsibilities), but also to the interests of others."
  o Law of Reciprocity: Matthew 7:12 "So in everything, do to others what you would have them do to you, for this sums up the Law and the Prophets."

- **Grace that Forgives – Ephesians 4:31-32**
  o **Release the resentment** (χάριζομάί) – Eph. 4:32 "Be kind and compassionate to one another, forgiving each other, just as in Christ God forgave you."
  o A personal act by the offended that releases the resentment for a wrong done to him or her. God holds no resentment toward us and neither should we then toward others. It is a personal act that then, if possible, allows one to confront their offender and address the issue without a spirit of bitterness.
  o **Cancel the debt** (άφιημί) Luke 17:3-4 "If your brother sins, rebuke him, and if he repents, forgive him." Complete forgiveness where the debt is cancelled or the consequences for one's wrong doing are accepted, comes with the offender reaching a point of repenting first. This acceptance of the consequences or cancelling of one's indebtedness is conditioned on the offender repenting.

The Gratitude Strategy

Understanding His grace awakens in us an inner motivation of gratitude that empowers each of us to live as God intended man to live: Like Christ.

**Gratitude for Christ awakens my commitment to
love as He loves**

- "I couldn't have written the Script"

"Let's Make Music with what we have left." Itzhak Perlman - Lincoln Center 1995

"This is the day the Lord has made" (Ps. 118:24),
and again, the mere fact that we breathe means we are part of His plan for the day.
"...but the people who know their God will display strength and take action."
(Daniel 11:32-NASB)

Awakened to Grace

Gratitude awakens commitment; purpose, vision, goals and desires direct it. Priorities systematize commitment; devotion and endurance fulfill it, by awakening a gratitude for all He has done.

The Attitude of Gratitude

So let's make music together with what we have

left. Take-Away Thoughts

_____
_____
_____

Homework - Session 11

1. **Read Chapter 13 Let's Make Music** from *Caregivers: The Unsung Heroes of Our Day*. What additional thoughts or clarifications were helpful from the reading?

2. Gratitude awakens commitment. Even though many circumstances confronting the caregiver seem to be difficult, **take time to review what generates a grateful spirit in you.**
   - **Name one experience**, event or accomplishment that has passed the test of time to awaken your present life with thanksgiving.

   - Concentrating on your spouse and family, **what highlight can you recall** that surrounds them and which still stirs your heart with thanksgiving?

3. **Take time for some stimulating conversation with your spouse or family members.** Ask how a sense of God's grace and a spirit of gratitude have shaped their motivations for life, especially in light of the disability and call to caregiving.
(Be prepared for the pain that such honesty can bring, especially if, in the process of handling adversity, the ones sharing have not progressed beyond handling the effects and challenges that accompany them.) **Jot down your results.**

4. **Read Chapter 14 A Touch of Hope: Communion with God** from *Caregivers: The Unsung Heroes of Our Day.* What additional thoughts or clarifications were helpful from the reading?

The real "touch of hope" which offers the greatest source of confidence in our inner being comes from one's personal "communion with God." One step in that communion reminds each of us to preach the gospel or good news about Christ to ourselves daily. This exercise is designed to expand our sense of gratitude. We are forgiven, and the sense of gratitude that accompanies this truth compels us to greater heights and mobilizes us to action. *May your understanding of Christ's work on our behalf be a real source of daily refreshment!*

- How has the thought that God seeks to relate to you personally affected your life and relationship with Him?

- Recognizing that we are sinners is not a difficult task to accomplish. Accepting that we have sinned and that sin brings us under its curse of separation from God puts a whole different outlook on our relationship with God, both in this world and the world to come. Communion with God, which involves preaching the gospel (good news of Christ) to ourselves daily, implies that we have reached a point in our lives in which we have surrendered to God and have accepted His gift of new life. Our relationship with Him is restored through our prayerful acceptance of Christ as our Lord and Savior. **When did that relationship begin for you?**

- **If this has not occurred, please take the time now** to ask the Lord to come into your life, forgive your sins that He paid the price for on the cross. Ask Him to restore your relationship with Him as your Lord. Tell someone that you trust about your new commitment and your new pursuit to become a child of God and a follower of Jesus Christ.

- Take time to reflect just how much He has forgiven you. Has a spirit of gratitude begun to awaken in you?

Session 12:
The Power of Caregiving

Notes

The Power of Caregiving

> "'My grace is sufficient for you, for my power is made perfect in weakness.'
> Therefore, I will boast all the more gladly about my weaknesses, so that Christ's power may rest on me."
> *II Corinthians 12:9*

Caregivers: Angels of kindness
- **Often pushed to the limits**
- **The sign of the crocus**
- **Caregiving: A way of life**

- Do you see it? If you look you can't miss it. It's the way of the caregiver who is honest with life and Almighty God. It's the way of the Master Caregiver that I have found my life begin to emulate, because through the storm He never stopped being Lord of All. His love and care for our weakest moments, through us into others, reflects again how "His power is perfected."

- What I had become was because all along the way His guiding hand had drawn out of me that same compassion that He has shown to us all. It enabled me to see people as God sees them, all with flaws but bearing His image and in turn to be to them that "very present help in trouble," regardless of its cost.

- Over the years, compassion began its expression in me to my own surprise, as God began drawing out of my inmost being to help the helpless, especially my wife.

Caregivers willingly give, not for what they receive in return, but because it is what is honorable and right before God and man.

Once caregivers accept their place, their lives transform. This brings with it an atmosphere that communicates to others that life around them is safe. Genuine love, which one did not earn and which one knows cannot be lost, fills the air.

When caregivers direct their skills toward those who also happen to be our dearest and closest friends, even our trusted confidants and family, a gratitude awakens new each day.

The Caregiver's Secret
Caring! That is what caregivers do. Care!

- How unique that in the crucible of pain and suffering, a powerful display of God is revealed—a transforming power that draws out of its crushed objects a characteristic that could not be obtained, apart from a face-to-face confrontation with evil or the ugliness a fallen world throws upon its inhabitants.
- Yet, here the power of unfailing love gains the potential to be at its best. Here the power of God Himself interweaves His compassionate hand and mercy that draws each caregiver to action.

The secret to the power of caregiving:

God at work in man, doing what God does best, transforming man to be like Him.

The Caregiver's Secret Mantra

What care I who gets the credit,
Only let the work be done,
God Himself will handle credit
With the setting of the sun.
People praise you, people blame you;
Rise above it everyday,
For soul, you will never win a battle,
If you fear what men may say.

A Special Thanks
- Matt Randall and Laura Jane -
- Beth Armstrong and Travis -
- Josh Randall and Karen -
- Marjie Randall -

There are not enough nice and good words to say about their actions and the love that they have expressed as caregivers, which has spanned most of their lives. Indeed, these are the heroes of our day whom I hold in great esteem and thanks.

To all those who find themselves in the cycle of caregiving, I tip my hat. Our country is great because of the compassion that is often learned and expressed by those who are marked by being caregivers.

Thank you for making a difference that matters.

Layout for the Last Session
Dessert time: Start the session by taking time to enjoy dessert. **Everyone needs to bring his favorite dessert to this session.** As the goodies are enjoyed, be prepared to interact about the material covered in the sessions.

1. Did you grasp the four corners to puzzling events and the cycle of adversity, and why it is so important to understand where another person finds himself or herself before trying to offer help?

2. Can you place yourself in that cycle?

3. How has your understanding of God been enriched by the opportunity to see God in yourself as you encounter the arduous task of caregiving? Think of a personal illustration.

4. As the gospel not only redeems us from the curse of sin, which is separation from God, it also serves to evoke gratitude that acts as the great motivator for all of one's life. How personally has the relation with Our Lord affected your place as a caregiver (disabled or ill)?

5. What were some of the valuable lessons that you will take away from the class and group?

6. Who can you thank?

7. How has your relationship with God been affected by the class both from the content, your own study and private time with God, and by the relationships shared with others in the group? Have certain Scriptures become personalized or provided personal encouragement? If so, which ones and what caused them to become so precious?

The Next Step

- Remember, going through a course for a second time and building relationships with others who travel the same pathway has a way of enriching our souls. The first time through, we spend so much time trying to understand and relate to the material. The second time, the major ideas find reinforcement, and the little nuggets of gold that can be overlooked are picked up and ideas are solidified and thoughts expanded as we relate principles and ideas more precisely to our situations.

- Influencing others is always valuable. What friends do we have who would benefit from these interactions and friendships? Can we invite them to our next session and take them under our wings to mentor?

"Adieu" – for God

**Compassion's compelling sympathy and sorrow
for another's misfortunes and suffering
find completion only in their unrelenting desire
to alleviate or remove the source of such pain.**

Caregivers: The Unsung Heroes of Our Day

Support Group Registration Information

Name _____ M / F (circle one) Date _____
Address _____ Phone _____
City _____ Email: _____
State _____ Zip _____ Age _____
Home Church Name _____
    Address _____
        (city)   (state)   (zip)

Marital Status
- Married ( ) Spouse's name _____ How Long? _____
- Single ( )

Children (Names & Ages)

_____   _____
_____   _____
_____   _____

Information

Describe your situation as a caregiver. Give a brief history and time line of your journey to this point.

_____
_____
_____
_____
_____
_____
_____
_____
_____
_____
_____

What pressing questions are you facing as a caregiver (disabled, etc)?

_____
_____
_____
_____
_____

What have you read that has helped you handle your situation?

_____
_____
_____

How has your view of God been influenced by the situation that you face?

_____
_____
_____
_____
_____
_____
_____
_____
_____
_____
_____
_____
_____
_____
_____
_____

www.ingramcontent.com/pod-product-compliance
Lightning Source LLC
Chambersburg PA
CBHW060848050426
42453CB00008B/885